Miss Frances Emery
410 - 11th Ave. S. E.
Mpls
Minn.

1024 - 3rd Ave. So.
Fargo
N. D.

The Lady of the Portrait

From a painting by Sir Joshua Reynolds

THE BEAU OF BATH

AND OTHER ONE-ACT PLAYS
OF EIGHTEENTH CENTURY LIFE

BY

CONSTANCE D'ARCY MACKAY

AUTHOR OF

*"Costumes and Scenery for Amateurs," "Patriotic Plays and
Pageants," "The House of the Heart, and Other
Plays for Children," etc.*

ILLUSTRATED FROM PORTRAITS

NEW YORK
HENRY HOLT AND COMPANY
1915

PS
3525
A2479
B4
1 915

THE QUINN & BODEN CO. PRESS
RAHWAY, N. J.

PREFACE

THE one-act plays in verse which this volume contains are dramatic miniatures of some of the notables of the eighteenth century in England. All of the plays are of the same period. Therefore, if so desired, three or four of them may be given consecutively with no change of scene by the simple expedient of moving the furniture and having different lighting. Watteau-like screens, a clavier for a harpsichord, the right use of chintz and brocade, firelight, candlelight or moonlight skillfully managed, and the thing is done!

Little theatres, theatres intimes, and studio stages are constantly showing that atmosphere may be created by the most simple effects, whether for amateur or professional. And surely the atmosphere of no century can be conveyed more easily by a mere touch than that of the eighteenth, with its wits and belles, its powder and patches, its mannered elegance, its brocades and lace.

CONTENTS

ILLUSTRATIONS

THE BEAU OF BATH

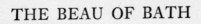

THE BEAU OF BATH

CHARACTERS

BEAU NASH
JEPSON, his servant
THE LADY OF THE PORTRAIT

PLACE: *Bath.*

TIME: *Christmas Eve, 1750.*

SCENE: *A room in the Beau's apartment.*

Furniture and hangings of faded splendor. Candles gleam in silver sconces. Christmas holly hangs here and there. At the left a fire burns on the hearth, first with small blue dancing flames, then deepening to a rosy glow.

At the right there is an inlaid desk with candles burning on it. Toward background a door opening into another room of the apartment.

In the center background hangs the life-sized portrait of a lady dressed in the fashion of the early eighteenth century. Her dress is a shimmer of rose-colored satin. Beneath her faintly powdered hair her face is young, dawn-tinted, starry-eyed. There are no other portraits in the room.

At the rise of the curtain Beau Nash is discovered seated at a round lacquered table, center foreground.

He is an old man, still very erect and stately, very much the great dandy. The soft light of the room hides whatever ravages of time there may be in his face. It also hides the fact that the seams of the black velvet suit he is wearing are growing gray, and that the creamy lace ruffles that grace his sleeves and jabot have been very often mended. Near him stands his servant, an old man slightly stooped, wearing a shabby brown cloth suit with a buff vest and tarnished gold buttons. He looks at his master adoringly.

JEPSON

And is that all, sir?

BEAU NASH

Bring my snuffbox. So!
Where are the cards?

JEPSON

(bringing a pack of cards on a silver tray).
Here, sir.

BEAU NASH

Now you may go.
(Jepson pauses).
You hesitate?

JEPSON

(with feeling).
Why, sir, I'm loath to see
You sitting here alone.

BEAU NASH
              This room, for me,
Is filled with memories.

JEPSON
              Aye, sir, I know.
I've served you thirty years and seen the flow
And ebb of fortune, and I cannot bear
Night after night to——

BEAU NASH
                    Jepson, all that's fair
Passes and fades.   Even the eagle's wings
Grow slow with age.   Content with little things
Is wisest.

> [*Jepson fetches a score pad and pencil from
> the desk, and stands waiting with them at
> his master's table.*

JEPSON
      Yes, sir.

BEAU NASH
(watching fire).
              See how strangely blue
The little flames are.   *If it should be true . . .*

JEPSON
(puzzled).
Sir?

BEAU NASH

That a spell is wrought by candle light
And gleaming flame when it shines faintly bright.
When hours grow small and embers lower burn
On Christmas night they say old loves return.
'Tis merely folly, Jepson. Ne'er again
Shall I behold that brilliant courtly train
Of wits and beauties, fops and gamesters gay—
All that made life in Bath when I held sway.
Time was, my nod would stop the Prince's dance:
A belle was made by my admiring glance:
'Twas I who set the fashions in brocade,
But—laurels wither and the roses fade,
And now I sit alone. My reign is done.
The wits and fops have vanished one by one.

JEPSON

(moved).

You were the King of all, sir. High and low
Admired you.

BEAU NASH

Thank you, Jepson.
(Takes score pad and pencil.)

You may go.
[*Exit Jepson, left, quietly and reluctantly, with
a backward glance at his master who still
dreams at fire.*

Everything passes. Naught remains of all
Except that portrait smiling from the wall.
[*He crosses to the portrait, candlestick in hand.*

Disdainful Rosamond, you still look down
As when you were the toast of all the town.
Lips red as holly, eyes so archly bright——
Nay, but your beauty dims the candle's light!

> [*He puts down the candlestick.*

'Tis vain to wish for things that may not be;
Yet could you for one hour come back to me
Would I not say all that I left unsaid
In days gone by? But you are long since dead,
While I, grown old, above the embers cower,

> [*He goes back to his chair.*

Or play a game to help me pass the hour
When shadows flicker . . . and the candles blink
Until I drowse . . . and . . .

> [*He nods and dozes in his chair. The Lady
> of the Portrait moves, smiles, slowly and
> gracefully steps down from the portrait,
> silently crosses to the table, her eyes on
> the Beau. She catches up a handful of
> cards.*

THE LADY

'Tis my play, I think
If I see rightly by the candle's gleam.

BEAU NASH
(in a whisper).

Rosamond!

THE LADY

(lightly).

Well, sir, do you always dream
When you play cards with ladies? If 'tis so
I think 'twere best to call my chair and go.

BEAU NASH

(bewildered, passing a hand across his eyes).

I thought . . . that you were dead . . . and I was old!

THE LADY

(still lightly).

Fie, sir, to think that hearts like ours grow cold!
And when I hear you call upon my name
Shall I not step down from that gilded frame
To spend an hour of Christmas night with you?
Come! Let us gossip of the folk we knew!
Lord Foppington, whose wit I did adore——

BEAU NASH

I thought Lord Foppington a monstrous bore!
But Kitty Cavendish—— 'Faith, one mad night
We drank her health from out her slipper white.

THE LADY

(with spirit).

I vow then you were tipsy, one and all,
For Kitty's slipper was by no means small.

BEAU NASH

Nay, let's have done with thrust and counter thrust!
Ah, Rosamond, in days gone by you must
Have known I loved you, yet you were so cold.

THE LADY
(very low).

I had been warmer, sir, had you been bold!

BEAU NASH

Bold! At your feet dukes laid their coronets,
I could but offer you some gambling debts.
These, and the worship of a world-worn heart
Would scarce pass coinage in Dame Fashion's mart.
So I fought down my love for you, and yet
Your slightest gesture in the minuet
Would stir my pulses. With a covert glance
I watched you through the mazes of the dance,
So fair, so radiant—— But what need for me
To tell you of my heart's poor comedy.
Is that a tear which falls for it, my sweet?

THE LADY
(very sweetly and gently).

A tear is naught, sir.
(She turns to him.)
Ah, must I repeat
My love in *words* before you will believe
That I too loved in vain?
(As their eyes meet her meaning grows clear to him.)
Now I must leave,
For 'tis not long until the clock strikes one.

Beau Nash

And you loved me!

The Lady

                    Our hour is almost done.
I leave you to your firelight and your chair,
And to your game that's always—solitaire!

> [*With delicate tread, moving silently as a ghost,
> the Lady steps back into the portrait. The
> Beau dozes again. The rosy glow of the fire
> dies, leaving the room in utter twilight.
> Jepson enters.*

Jepson

'Tis bedtime, sir.   The clock struck long ago.
The embers on the hearth are burning low.
Even the wav'ring candle feebly gleams.

Beau Nash

(with a startled glance about the shadowy room).

So late! . . . So dim! . . . I have been dreaming—
        Dreams!

THE CURTAIN SLOWLY FALLS

THE SILVER LINING

THE SILVER LINING

CHARACTERS

FANNY BURNEY
RICHARD BURNEY, her uncle
CEPHAS, an old servant
PLACE: *Chessington.*
TIME: *1778.*
SCENE: *Library in Mr. Crisp's house.*

A pleasant room, a trifle littered with books and papers. All across the background, windows curtained in palely flowered damask. A hearth at left, with a fire burning rosily. Brass andirons. A bellows. Near the hearth, facing audience, a dark-wooden settle with a high back. It is handsomely carved and appears to be quite old. Candles in silver candlesticks are lighted on the hearth shelf, and there are also framed silhouettes standing there.

At right, near background, a door opening into another room of the house. Also at left, towards foreground, a round table with a lighted candelabra, several drawings in striking black and white. A brass inkstand, sand, quill pens, etc. All along the right wall a dark bookcase full to running over with books. Its top shelf is piled high with them. Their covers are

*mostly brown and musty.   There are also black, dark
blue and green ones, but none in bright colors.*

*At the rise of the curtain Fanny Burney, rather
small, delicate, with a girlishly pretty face and softly
curling unpowdered hair sits writing at the table, a
small work-bag and sampler lying on her lap.   She
wears a pale yellow dress, flowered in white, over a
pale yellow petticoat, and a white lace fichu.   Black
velvet ribbon at her throat, and about her wrists.   She
is deep in her work when there is the sound of someone
opening the door at right.   With amazing swiftness
Fanny drops her pen, sweeps the drawings over what
she is writing, drops her sampler and bag on top of
them, and is crocheting when her uncle, Richard
Burney, enters.   He is a tall, portly, ruddy man, with
a most important manner.   He wears a handsome
plum-colored traveling suit, and carries a long church-
warden pipe which he lights without a "by your
leave" at his first opportunity.*

RICHARD BURNEY

Well, Fanny!

FANNY BURNEY
(surprised).

Uncle!

RICHARD BURNEY

Cephas welcomed me.
There's no one else about as I can see.
(Fanny drops a flurried curtsey.)
Where's Mrs. Gast?

FANNY BURNEY
                    In bed. And Daddy Crisp
Has gone to London.

RICHARD BURNEY
                    Cephas, with his lisp,
Has so informed me. And I also know
Your father left here just three days ago,
So I have missed him. Lord! What a to-do!
I'm just from town myself. Child, how are you?

FANNY BURNEY
(prettily).
Quite well, and hope my kinsfolk are the same.

RICHARD BURNEY
(puffing at his pipe before the fire).
Um. Yes.
                    FANNY BURNEY
                    What news?

RICHARD BURNEY
                    The whole town rings with fame
Of a new author, who has writ a book
Called " Evelina." Everywhere you look
You see it advertised. Yet no one knows
The author's name and rumor madly goes
Naming first this one, and then that one.

FANNY BURNEY

(passionately).

Oh,
If they should ever guess! *(She grows pale.)*

RICHARD BURNEY

They're sure to know
Sooner or later. Burke sat up all night
To read it. Said if he could guess aright
The author's name, that fifty pounds he'd give,
While Dr. Johnston cried out: "As I live
I can't forget the book. It's my delight!"
Why, Fanny! How you look! First red, then white.

FANNY BURNEY

(trying to speak without a tremor).

You see, in Chessington, our life is dull,
And everything you say seems wonderful,
And stirs the heart like bells of London town.
And so this—"Katherina" wins renown?

RICHARD BURNEY

Nay, "Evelina" so the novel's named.
The author who has written it is famed
Forever. 'Tis a puzzle. No one can
Be positive who is the lucky man.
If, when I've read it I have found 'twill do
For you to read, 'twill be permitted you.

FANNY BURNEY
(demurely).

Thank you.

RICHARD BURNEY
How's Charles?

FANNY BURNEY

And busy.   My father's vastly well,

RICHARD BURNEY
Humph. I think that I could tell
That without asking. Times are hard. I saw
A friend of Charles' last night—young Clapperclaw
Who swears that Clark wrote " Evelina." Fool!
But when I said 'twas more like Fielding's school
Mrs. Thrale looked at me the oddest way,
Said: *" Did you get the note I sent to-day?*
Go search for ' Evelina' nearer home.
If you would find her you've not far to roam."
(Fanny turns and looks at him, aghast; but he con-
tinues placidly.)
I think she means that Anstey's written it.
But, lord, I'm sure that he has not the wit!
Although the strangest people try to write:
Children and fools. I've not forgot the night
Your father found *you* at it, clipped your wing,
Forbade such nonsense and then burned the thing,
And brought you to your senses. Pen and ink
Are not for women, but for men who think.
Females are cackling geese. 'Tis only men
Who have the strength of mind to wield a pen.

FANNY BURNEY
(picking up pen from table).

And yet this pen is made from a goose feather!

RICHARD BURNEY
(frowning).

Well, pens and women do not go together.
A bluestocking is a disgrace. *(Yawns.)* Heigho!
The hour grows late. I'll take my candle.

> [*He crosses to table, takes candle, and pauses
> to pick up drawings for inspection. As he
> lifts one it catches on the manuscript beneath,
> and the latter sweeps to the floor, and falls
> with pages outspread.*

FANNY BURNEY
(with a stifled exclamation).

Oh!

RICHARD BURNEY
(puzzled; then angry).

What's this? *(Picks up a few pages.)* Great heavens!
Fanny! Well, I swear
You *have* been writing! And you've hid it there
Behind your sampler. Wait till Charles hears this!

FANNY BURNEY
(imploring him).

Oh, Uncle Richard, if you'll——

RICHARD BURNEY
                              Silence, miss!
You should be shamed to look me in the face.
Thank God that no one else knows this disgrace.
How far has this thing gone?   Come, answer me.
Who else has seen this rubbish besides me?

FANNY BURNEY
(terrified).

Oh, Uncle——

RICHARD BURNEY
(with mounting rage).
                      Wait till Charles and I confer!

Who else?

FANNY BURNEY
(between sobs).
I've sent it to a publisher.

RICHARD BURNEY
(furiously).

Fanny!   Don't tell me you have been so bold!

FANNY BURNEY
(sobbing wildly).

Oh,—worse—than—that!   *The—book's—already—
        sold!*

RICHARD BURNEY
(starting violently).

Sold! Why, God bless me! Fanny, you don't say
That you got money for it? *(He stares at her, open-
mouthed.)*

FANNY BURNEY
(with a fresh burst of tears).

Yes, to-day
A—check—came——

RICHARD BURNEY
(eagerly).

For how much?

FANNY BURNEY
(choked with sobs).

Two—hundred—pounds.*

RICHARD BURNEY
(staggered).

Two hun—— Why, Fanny! I am dreaming! Zounds!
When did you write?

FANNY BURNEY
(struggling for self-control).

A little, every day.
I covered it with samplers and crochet.
(She wipes her eyes.)

* This is a slight exaggeration for the sake of dramatic effectiveness.

RICHARD BURNEY
(quite mollified).

What's the book called?

FANNY BURNEY
(trembling).
'Tis " Evelina."

RICHARD BURNEY
(stunned).

You
Wrote " Evelina "? *(Fanny nods.)* Lord! What a
to-do!
When Burke hears this! That Clapperclaw's a fool!
(With triumph.)
I knew the book came from some other school!
(Expands as if talking to imaginary people.)
" My niece, the authoress . . ."

FANNY BURNEY
(approaching him humbly).
Uncle, I know
I've been deceitful, but I loved it so—
My book. Forgive me. I won't write again.

RICHARD BURNEY
Eh? Oh, tut, tut! I wouldn't cause you pain
For your—er—fault.

FANNY BURNEY
(with emotion).

Uncle, if you could dream
All that it meant to me, the thrill—the gleam—
You'll never guess what dull hours I've beguiled.

RICHARD BURNEY
(patronizingly).

There! There! Remember you're my niece, dear child.
One mustn't be too hard on what's one's own.

FANNY BURNEY
(with quick gratitude).

Oh, *Uncle!*

RICHARD BURNEY
(condescendingly).

If you want to be alone
Sometimes, and write, I've no objection—none.

FANNY BURNEY
(radiant).

Uncle!

RICHARD BURNEY
(to himself).

And when I think how quick it's done——
Just write a book, and make two hundred pounds!

    [*Cephas appears at door right, an old man in
        snuff-colored livery. He carries a candle,
        and an iron ring with some large keys on it.*

CEPHAS

Miss Fanny——

FANNY BURNEY

(to her uncle).

Cephas wants to make his rounds
And lock the doors.

RICHARD BURNEY

Then, child, good night.

[*Fanny takes a candle from the table. Motions to Cephas to go. He exits, right, and Fanny drops a curtsey to her uncle.*

FANNY BURNEY

Good night.

RICHARD BURNEY

(intercepting her).

You think that you might write some more as bright
As " Evelina "?

FANNY BURNEY

(modestly).

I can try.

RICHARD BURNEY

Yes, do.

[*Again Fanny etches him a dutiful curtsey. He smiles at her benignly between puffs of smoke as he stands with his back to the fire.*

She exits, right, with her candle. Richard
Burney puffs complacently, yet with the air
of a man who must speak aloud in order to
give vent to his feelings. His sentences come
between enjoyable whiffs.

RICHARD BURNEY

Well, even if the hussy's socks *are* blue
She's my own niece. One shouldn't be repining
To find blue stockings have a silver lining.
The little baggage! Lord! Two hundred pounds!
Well, Charles can spend it fixing up his grounds!

QUICK CURTAIN

ASHES OF ROSES

ASHES OF ROSES

CHARACTERS

KITTY CLIVE
HORACE WALPOLE
PHYLLIS
ROXANE, maid to Mistress Clive
Call Boy

PLACE: *London.*

TIME: *A Spring night in 1741.*

SCENE: *The theatre dressing-room of Kitty Clive.*

The bare white-washed walls of the dressing-room are almost hidden by the softly tinted costumes that hang from their pegs. There are also shimmering cloaks, a wig or so. A mask and domino. A mock-ermine robe. In background, right, a door with a light cloak hanging on it. When this door is opened, the dingy backs of stacked scenery show dimly. Against the wall of left background a spindle-legged dressing table glittering with silver paste boxes, brushes, smell-ing salts bottles, powder boxes, all of which are reflected with double glitter in the mirror that hangs above them. Lighted candles in silver sconces jut from each side of the mirror. There are six candles in each sconce, and their illumination falls like a soft glory

over the room. There are two damask chairs with
gilt legs, one for Kitty Clive, and one for any chance
visitor. The one for Kitty Clive is in front of the
dressing table. The other stands near and is covered
with a frou-frou of stage dresses.

At the rise of the curtain Kitty Clive is seated at the
table with Roxane in attendance. The actress is
sumptuous in blue and silver brocade, worn over a
white satin petticoat. Her hair is dressed very high,
and is white with powder. A necklace of pearls and
diamonds glitters about her throat. Her cheeks and
lips are rouged. Her great eyes sparkle under pen-
ciled eyebrows. Her hands are thick with rings.
On her white satin high-heeled slippers flash the most
brilliant of buckles. Her white silk stockings have
silver clocks. Roxane, a slim, sprightly creature, wears
an old rose dress looped over an old rose and white-
striped petticoat. A white kerchief and a frilled white
cap on her dark hair. A saucy white apron. She holds
a hare's foot mounted in silver and a silver patch box.

CLIVE

Quick with the hare's foot! Lud, your hands are slow!
Nay, I spoke sharply. Next the patches. So!
Fasten this bit of ribbon to the right,
And set this diamond crescent well in sight.
Then for this side-wise curl more powder bring.
How look I now?

ROXANE

Mistress, as fair as Spring.

CLIVE

" As fair as Spring! "   God, what an age ago
Since Spring and I were friends!   I used to know
The banks whereon the early violets grew
Lifting their little faces deeply blue——
Yet not more deeply blue than a lad's eyes
In those sweet days ere town had made me wise,
Ere I had learned that flattery hides a dart,
And fame feeds vanity, but not the heart. . . .
Oh, those far days. . . .

(She speaks more to herself than to Roxane.)

ROXANE

(as a rap sounds on the door).

Mistress!

CLIVE

(rousing herself).

'Tis Walpole's rap.

Bid him come in.

> [*Roxane opens the door.   Walpole enters, a
> distinguished-looking man with great charm
> of manner.   He wears a suit of gray satin
> with the customary ruffles and flowered
> waistcoat.   His tri-corn hat is tucked under
> his arm.   His powdered wig is almost as
> elaborate as that of Clive herself.*

I knew you by your tap!

> [*She does not rise, but extends her hand, which
> he kisses gallantly.*

WALPOLE

My tap is ever at the *Queen and Star.*

CLIVE

Fie, Horace! What a flatterer you are!
How many occupations you must fit
To start as tapster, and to end as wit!
A courtier also!

WALPOLE

Never that with you.

CLIVE

(to Roxane).

Go wait, Roxane, and call me ere my cue.

[*Exit Roxane. Clive turns to Walpole with
genuine feeling.*

My deep, true friend. There are not many such.

WALPOLE

Pensive, sweet Kit?

CLIVE

(affecting to be busy with powder puff and hare's foot).

Nay, Horace, 'tis the touch
Of an old sadness that the waking year
Wakes in my heart. We mouthe and stutter here,
Snatching such tinsel as the town may fling,
While out beyond the city it is Spring . . .

Spring in the country lanes where lovers stray,
Spring! And the Devon hedgerows white with May!
Hedgerows of Devon! *(Turns to Walpole.)* Friend,
    there used to be
A lad who walked in those green lanes with me
And spoke of love. But I—I heard the town
Calling me with a voice that would not down.
I heard. I followed. London gave me fame,
And all has changed since then—my life, my name.
And yet I think I never can forget
The garden where we parted. It was set
With sweetbriar roses. 'Faith, I know not why
I tell you fragments of a day gone by,—
Save that he said: "Dearheart, lest you return,
A light shall ever in that window burn
Through all the years." He had no subtle art,
My country lover. Yet, against my heart
To-night—his rose! *(Takes a faded rose from the
    bosom of her dress.)*
                  Oh, Horace, you who know
How vain and false and empty is the show,
How foul the fawning, and how barbed the wit,
Think me not mad to say farewell to it——!
To quit the footlights for that candle's gleam,
To seek that simple faith of which I dream,
And find that the world lost for love is best——

ROXANE
(rapping briskly and then entering).

Mistress, a country zany, strangely dressed,
Would speak with you. She comes from Devon way.

CLIVE

(instantly interested).

From Devon? Bid her enter.

WALPOLE

(rising).

I'll not stay.

Adieu, sweet Clive.

CLIVE

(to herself).

From Devon!

*(Suddenly perceives that Walpole is going, and etches
him an abstracted curtsey.)*

Oh, adieu!

[*Exit Walpole. Enter Phyllis, a young girl,
with a sweet, rustic look. She wears a pale
yellow muslin dress, faintly sprigged with
white and a little pale yellow straw poke
bonnet, with pale yellow strings tied under
her chin. Long lace mitts. A little white
woolen cloak with swansdown edging. From
beneath the shade of her poke bonnet her eyes
look out with child-like earnestness. She re-
gards Clive with timid awe.*

PHYLLIS

My name is Phyllis. May I speak with you?

CLIVE

(looking at her with great interest).

Aye, child. Speak freely.

PHYLLIS

(shyly eager).

                        Last night at the play
I watched you. 'Twas so wondrous. You could sway
The house to tears or laughter, swift as flame!
And so (though father knows it not) I came
To-night to ask your counsel. You who know
The secrets of the heart—its joy, its woe——

> [*Clive's first interest has waned a little. She
> goes on with her toilet, yet speaks very kindly
> and patiently to Phyllis.*

CLIVE

Speak, child. But give me not too hard a task.

PHYLLIS

(gaining courage).

Oh, Mistress, 'tis not for myself I ask!
'Tis for a friend——

CLIVE

(absorbed with the art of her patch box).

                        A friend——

PHYLLIS

(hurriedly).

He lives alone
In a thatched cottage that is near our own,
And has a curious, rambling garden set
With sweetbriar roses——

CLIVE

(momentarily startled: then recovering herself).

Roses? I forget——
Proceed, my child.

PHYLLIS

(with courage).

And by a windowpane
Each night, for years, through starlight and through
rain
Has shone a lighted candle.

CLIVE

(motionless).

Ah!

PHYLLIS

(artlessly).

They say
That years ago his true love went her way
To London town: and lest she should return
And find the way all dark, he needs must burn
That welcome gleam. Though she was fain to roam
He felt that beacon light would guide her home.

CLIVE
(deeply moved).

Home!

PHYLLIS
(timidly).

Was it not a tender thing to do?

CLIVE
(deeply).

Aye.

PHYLLIS
(ardently).

Oh, there seldom beats a heart so true.
He loved her always.

CLIVE
*(in a thrilled voice, staring a-dream at something
Phyllis does not see).*

Always . . .!

PHYLLIS

Until now.

Mistress, indeed I scarce can tell you how
He came to care for me, his neighbor's child.
I doubted that he meant it. But he smiled
And said that after storm came peace and rest.
Great loves flamed high, but simple loves were best,
And sound of children's voices and a fire
Lit on the hearth for Autumn days—— I tire
You with my selfish chatter, Mistress?

CLIVE

(her face a mask).

Nay.

(searchingly.)

You love him?

PHYLLIS

(with genuine passion).

Oh, more deep than words can say!
Yet ever through my heart there runs a fear—
If we were wed, that love of yester-year
Might sometime lift the latch, and put to flight
His heart's deep peace—set memory's torch alight—
Re-ope the old wound, and the old, old pain——

CLIVE

(after a moment).

You need not fear—she'll not return again.

PHYLLIS

You think she will not—you who are so wise
In the world's ways and see with such clear eyes—
You think she will not?

CLIVE

(faintly smiling).

I am quite, quite sure.

PHYLLIS

(radiantly).

Oh, Mistress, for such counsel words are poor
To give in thanks.

CLIVE

*(rising wearily, her face beneath its paint suddenly
grown old).*

Nay, child. No thanks, I pray.
But sometimes . . . when the year is white with
   May . . .
Remember me.

> [*Phyllis suddenly bends and kisses Clive's hand,
> shyly impulsive and adoring. Clive lays the
> other hand for a moment gently on the girl's
> shoulder, looking at the youth of her, and
> then dismisses her with a light imperious
> gesture.*

Now go, child.

> [*Exit Phyllis.*

CALL BOY'S VOICE

(without).

Ready, all!

ROXANE

(entering breathlessly and with importance).

Mistress, they wait. It is the curtain call—
The curtain call—— And there's the prompter's
   bell——!

CLIVE

[*Looking at a faded sweetbriar rose which she
has taken from the bosom of her dress, and
which now crumbles to dust under her touch,
sifting like ashes through her fingers to the
floor.*

Strange—for a moment since the curtain fell!

CURTAIN

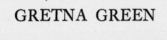

GRETNA GREEN

Miss Linley

After the portrait by Humphrey

GRETNA GREEN

CHARACTERS

MARIA LINLEY (secretly betrothed to Richard Brinsley Sheridan)
THOMAS LINLEY, her father
AVIS LINLEY, her aunt

PLACE: *Bath.*

TIME: *1772.*

SCENE: *The Linleys' home.*

A room that is a trifle shabby, furnished in the eighteenth century manner. Spindle-legged chairs upholstered in faded damask.

In the center background a door opening on the road without. Windows each side of it curtained with pale blue muslin flowered with pink roses. Under the window at right a spinet with music on the open rack, and piles of music placed on top of the spinet itself.

At left a hearth with a fire burning. Toward background a door.

At right, against the wall, an inlaid spindle-legged writing desk and chair.

Toward the center of the room, left, and facing audience, a winged chair upholstered in flowered chintz.

41

*Toward the center of the room, right, also facing
audience, a chintz-covered spindle-legged chair.*

*At the rise of the curtain Avis Linley is seated with
a sampler in her hand on chair, left, while near her
at right, sits Maria Linley, with a book in her hand.
Branched candlesticks on hearthshelf and spinet shed
a soft radiance over the room. From outside the
Autumn wind is heard blowing in fitful gusts.*

*Avis Linley, who has fallen asleep over her work,
is a woman of almost fifty, slender and upright as a
willow wand. Her hair, faintly touched with gray,
waves over a broad white brow. Her face, clear-cut
as a cameo, is faintly tinged with pink. She wears a
dress of pale blue chintz opening over a white petticoat.
Maria Linley, her niece, has her aunt's clear-cut cameo-
like features, the same delicate flush on her face. She
is young, charming, and in spite of her success in public,
rather diffident, with the manner of one who stands
in positive fear of her elders. She is reading aloud as
the curtains rise, and her voice suggests the singer. It
is full, sweet, resonant. She wears a white dress flowered in scarlet roses, over a scarlet quilted petticoat.
Her dark hair is unpowdered.*

MARIA

(reading).

*But all this happened very long ago
In Greece's golden age, when to and fro*

Walked nymphs and shepherds, Phyllis, Corydon,
And strange cold elves on whom the pale moon
shone——

> [*She pauses. Then in the same low musical*
> *voice essays to call her aunt, leaning forward*
> *half-timidly as she does so.*

Aunt Avis! Oh, Aunt Avis. She's asleep!
Perhaps if I go droning on she'll keep
So. But how can I read when thoughts roam far!
Oh, let my pent heart speak the things that are—
And substitute my own words for this book.

> [*She still holds the book, and continues to speak*
> *lullingly, as if she still read aloud.*

The lines all run together when I look.
I will pretend to read and lull her sleep,
Nor dare to stop. Have I the strength to creep
Up to my room, and there prepare to go?
I never knew an hour to pass so slow!
And Richard said we were to meet at ten
And take the chaise for Gretna Green. Or then
If that should fail, we'll cross the sea to France.
And either way 'tis Richard and Romance!
Poor Aunt! *(Looks at her.)* What lover ever sighed
    for her?
I'm sure she never felt the least, least stir
Of joy, or hope. Why all her time is spent
In making elder wine, or liniment,
Or playing on the harpsichord some tune
As faded as herself. I think she'd swoon

If she could guess what is a-foot to-night.
Or else she'd tell my father. That's a plight
That I grow pale to think on. Nay, 'tis time
That I were going——! *(Clock strikes.)* There's
    the half-hour's chime

    (Looks cautiously at her aunt.)

And aunt still sleeps! Well, those who love must dare.
I can creep past again behind her chair
And lift the latch as quiet as a mouse.

    (She puts down her book, after rising quietly.)

Listen! There's not a stir in all the house!
Father must be a-bed. I'll fetch my cloak.

> [*She pauses, center. Her aunt still sleeps
> soundly. Watching her, with great caution
> Maria tiptoes to the door at left, and exits.
> For a moment her aunt continues to slumber,
> then slowly opens her eyes, drowsily stifles
> a yawn, and speaks sleepily.*

Avis

Child, did I doze?

> [*Hearing no answer she looks at Maria's vacant
> chair, and speaks with the confusion of sleep
> still upon her.*

            I thought that someone spoke!
I must have dreamed it. *(Yawns drowsily.)* Though
    the wind blows drear
The Autumn stars shine frostily, and clear. . . .

[*She rises, takes her work, and pauses to look
out the window at right. Maria steals in on
tiptoe, ready for departure. She is fastening a
scarlet cloak with a hood, and does not per-
ceive her aunt till she is almost at the outer
door.*

AVIS

Child!

MARIA
(*greatly startled*).

Why, Aunt Avis!

AVIS

Can I trust my sight!
That hood! That cloak! And at this time of night!

MARIA
(*faltering*).

I do protest 'twas but to take the air
For a brief moment.

AVIS
(*with meaning*).

Or a coach and pair.

MARIA
(*aghast: faltering*).

A coach—and—— Oh, Aunt Avis! Who has told?

Avis

(composedly).

Why, no one, child. I am not yet too old
To read the signs where signs are to be seen,
And this sign plainly points to Gretna Green.

Maria

(to herself: more and more amazed).

To Gretna Green! And yet she does not swoon!

Avis

(quietly).

'Tis well you chose a night without a moon.
Yet why go thus?

Maria

(on the verge of tears).

              There was no other way;
For Richard spoke to father yesterday.
I listened, trembling, and my father said
That he would never see his daughter wed
To anyone as portionless and poor
As Richard Sheridan. *(Sobs.)* Or so *obscure*.

Avis

And was this all?

Maria

            Yes, all. Naught else I swear.
So it was either Gretna, or despair.
Dick said: " At ten! " And I could not refuse——

AVIS

The chaise——! At ten! Then you've no time to lose!

MARIA
(utterly bewildered).

" *No time to lose——!* " Oh, she's gone quite, quite
mad!

> [*Avis crosses swiftly to desk. Opens drawer.*
> *Takes out a jeweled trinket and money.*
> *Crosses to her niece.*

AVIS

Here, child, is a small trinket that I had
When I was young. 'Tis for a wedding gift.
And these few sovereigns may make a rift
Of cheerful sunshine on some rainy day.

MARIA
(with passionate gratitude).

Aunt Avis!

> [*A step is heard at left.*

AVIS

Nay, be quick! You must not stay!
Your father's coming. Kiss me, child. Adieu!
All my heart's love and blessings go with you.

> [*Exit Maria, center. Avis has just time to*
> *snatch up her work when Thomas Linley*
> *enters. He is a lordly person in a suit of*

dark brown velvet.   He crosses at once to fire.

LINLEY

Zounds!   Not in bed yet, Avis?

(He stands, rubbing his hands.)

We'll have snow.

(yawns.)

On such a night—full thirty years ago—
Do you remember—you were fain to run
To Gretna with that linen draper's son?

AVIS

Yes, I remember.

LINLEY

(with self-satisfaction).

And I stopped the chaise,
And brought you back.

AVIS

To empty, loveless days.

Yes, I remember.

LINLEY

(yawning).

Where's Maria?

AVIS

(with subdued fire).

Safe!

LINLEY
(a bit startled).

What do you mean?

AVIS

Why, brother, how you chafe
At the *least* word.   Where *should* Maria be?

LINLEY

Lord, the young baggage dares not cope with me!
I'm master of my own.
(There comes the sound of wheels passing without.)

Zounds, Avis!   Hark!
What's that without?

AVIS

The wind wails through the dark.

LINLEY

But I heard sounds above the wind's shrill cry.

AVIS

Naught but the post chaise, brother, passing by.

QUICK CURTAIN

COUNSEL RETAINED

Edmund Burke

From the portrait by George Romney

COUNSEL RETAINED

CHARACTERS

Peg Woffington
Richard Greville
Edmund Burke
Some unseen gallants, admirers of Peg Woffington
    Place: *London.*
     Time: *1750. A cold Spring night.*
     Scene: *The apartment of Edmund Burke.*

A room that gives evidence of extreme poverty. It is on the ground floor of what was once a fine mansion, but is now a lodging-house dreary and down-at-heel. At background, left, a French window with rusty lock and broken panes, one of which is stuffed with an old hat. At right background a couch with a faded and tattered damask cover.

At left center a hearth with a low fire. Andirons. A battered iron kettle on a hob. A dilapidated hearth-broom. Drawn near the hearth and facing audience a highbacked chair with arms, the remains of what was once a fine carved piece of furniture. Tossed over the back of it a lawyer's black gown, very frayed.

At right, near background, a door opening into the hall of the house. Near foreground a cupboard with a few dishes, etc.

In the center of the room a black table with an iron strong box, a pile of battered law books, briefs, port-folios, papers. A chair drawn up to the right of this.

On the table and mantelshelf are stubs of candles, two in battered pewter candlesticks, and one in the neck of a bottle.

At the rise of the curtain the room is in absolute darkness, save for the red spark of the fire burning jewel-like in the gloom. A moment afterwards a hand from without tries the lock of the French window, and wrenches the window open. A woman in a dark cloak enters quickly, and lets in a flood of Spring moonlight that falls in a broad shaft across the floor. She has no time to close the window, but steps quickly into the shadows by the fire, and stands silent and motionless, her face hidden by the hood of her cloak. From outside comes an excited tumult of men's voices.

First Voice

Peg! Mistress Woffington!

> [*Richard Greville steps through the window, a fine-looking young dandy in king's blue velvet, with white wig, small sword, flashing shoe-buckles. He gives a quick look about him, does not perceive the hooded figure and speaks back through the window.*

GREVILLE
                    She isn't here.
(With another quick glance at the room.)
Some pettifogger's lodgings. Gad! It's clear
That she won't let us chair her through the town.

VOICES
(without).

Huzzah for Woffington!

FIRST VOICE
                    Come on!

SECOND VOICE
                              We'll drown
Our ardor at the *Crown* or *Serpentine.*
  [*This is hailed with a cheer that instantly
    grows fainter as its givers move rapidly away.*

WOFFINGTON
(with involuntary indignation).
What! Will they drown my memory in wine!

GREVILLE
(surprised and entranced).
Peg!

WOFFINGTON

(sharply).

S-sh, I tell you! I will not be found.
Wait till they leave. I'm weary of this round
Of cheering and of torchlight. Let me be.

> [*As she sinks into the chair near hearth the
> moonlight shows her wonderful mobile face.
> The sparkle of excitement and the immortal
> youth of the artist make her look younger
> than she really is. She gives the effect of
> being not more than two and twenty. Her
> thin black silk hooded cloak lined in flame-
> scarlet satin falls back and reveals that over
> a black taffeta petticoat she wears an over-
> dress of black gauze on which are thickly em-
> broidered broad love-knots of silver. She has
> a black lace scarf caught with a huge scarlet
> rose. Above the darkness of her dress her
> neck rises superbly white. She wears no
> jewels. Her dark hair is unpowdered. Her
> little slippers are of the finest make, and
> rest lightly on the ground like two black but-
> terflies. They are without buckles.*

GREVILLE

(bending over her).

Why, Peg! Sweet Woffington!

WOFFINGTON

(closing her eyes for a moment and leaning back
wearily in the chair).

        Ah, can't you see
An actress may grow tired? I'm fagged to death!

(Sudden impish humor lights her face. She opens her
eyes.)

Besides, you know, I wish to save my breath.
I want a *little* left with which to speak.
My case against Miss Spleen comes off next week.

GREVILLE

Gad! So it does. I'm stupid to forget.
Have you engaged your counsel?

WOFFINGTON

        Nay, not yet.
Sure, Mr. Greville, I have had no time.
    (Sagely.)
But I'll be ready when the hour shall chime.

GREVILLE

Who will you take?

WOFFINGTON
(with a gleam).

       'Faith, set your mind at rest.
I'll choose the one who can defend me best!
Be sure of that.

GREVILLE

How did you *come* here?

WOFFINGTON

I

Stepped in to let the crowd go sweeping by,
And did what women can do when they will.

GREVILLE

And what was that?

WOFFINGTON
(with a deliberate brogue).

I managed to keep still!

GREVILLE
(glancing scornfully about the room).
Who do you think can own this—caravan?

WOFFINGTON

Sure, I don't know. It must be some poor man
Who's having a hard time to make things meet.
Well, may kind fortune set him on his feet!
I was poor once. *(Pensively.)*

VOICES
(in distance, without).
Huzzah!

WOFFINGTON

              I must stay here
Until the streets without begin to clear.
Fetch me a chair. Come back in half an hour.
Meanwhile I'll rest.

GREVILLE

          I will obey.

WOFFINGTON

(slight brogue).

              More power
To you, Dick Greville.

    [*Greville smiles delightedly, kisses her hand,
        and exits through French window, which he
        half closes, so that Woffington is left partly
        in light, partly in shadow. The moment he
        is gone a key turns in the lock of the door,
        right. Woffington starts, looks towards door,
        and draws her cloak about her prepared for
        flight if flight prove necessary. Edmund
        Burke enters, young, shabby, careworn, wear-
        ing a black suit and a black cloak seen sharply
        for a moment as he takes a flint from his
        pocket and tries to strike a light. He has
        not seen Woffington, who instantly draws his
        old gown about her, and slips her arm into
        its sleeves. She stoops forward, rubs her
        handkerchief in the ash that has sifted out
        beyond the hearth, puts a smirch of it on her*

*hands, tucks her feet under her, and hud-
dling deep in the chair assumes a forlorn
look, closing her eyes. She has slyly managed to pick up the hearth broom, and it lies
against her knee. She might, seen in the
shadow, be a crossing sweeper, instead of an
actress. Meanwhile Burke has lighted the
stump of candle standing in the neck of a
bottle. As soon as it is lit he looks about
and sees Woffington.*

BURKE
(astonished).
What is this?

WOFFINGTON
*(with the effect of astonishment, bewilderment, the
"Where am I" look of a person just wakened).*
Why, oh!——

*(She looks at him in consternation, pretends to gather
her wits together. Speaks coaxingly, as one afraid
of a reprimand.)*

There was a crowd outside, and so—and so——
I stepped in here a moment, and 'twas warm,
And I dozed off——

BURKE
I'm sure you meant no harm.

[*He crosses, closes the window, but does not
try to lock it. Then goes to hearth and*

*lights the stumps of candles on the hearth-
shelf.*

WOFFINGTON

(very Irish throughout).

None in the least, sir.

BURKE

And your name is——

WOFFINGTON

Meg

Some people call me, and the others Peg.
I like Meg best.

[*She looks at him with the engagingness of a
gamin.*

BURKE

(kindly).

Well, Meg, I greatly fear
That I can only offer you small cheer.

WOFFINGTON

I don't mind that.

BURKE

Stale bread, stale cheese, scant light.

[*He has crossed to cupboard, right, and while
he goes on talking to her sets between them
on the table cracked plates, a loaf of bread,
and some cheese.*

What do you do?

WOFFINGTON

(with an inspiration).

   I—sweep the boards at night!

BURKE

A crossing sweeper?

WOFFINGTON

(looking down on his cloak).

   'Faith, I know 'twas bold
To take this cloak: but I was tired and cold,
And I——

BURKE

(with a whimsical glance at his supper table).

   Ah, the poor know the poor. Sit still.

WOFFINGTON

You're very kind.

BURKE

   I know how night can chill
The very marrow.

WOFFINGTON

   Are you Irish, too?

BURKE

Yes.

WOFFINGTON
(slowly).

If it's not—asking too much of you
What is your name, sir?

BURKE
Burke.   Unknown to fame.
Just Edmund Burke.

WOFFINGTON
(sagely).

That's a good Irish name.
And it will bring you luck.   Now, tell me true,
What do you need most?

BURKE
Clients.   One or two
Friends in the great world.

WOFFINGTON
Have you none?

BURKE
Nay, none.

WOFFINGTON
(encouragingly).

Keep up your heart.   Perhaps you'll meet with one.

BURKE
(kindly).

Why, thank you, Meg.

WOFFINGTON
You're welcome.

BURKE
(bowing).

Will you share
My bread and cheese? *(They begin to eat.)*

WOFFINGTON
You offer me your fare
As if I were a lady!
BURKE
Aren't you?
Isn't a lady one whose words ring true
From a kind heart?

WOFFINGTON
There's Mistress Woffington—
She's kind, they say, and yet she isn't one.

BURKE
(indulgently).

Isn't a lady?
WOFFINGTON
You have seen her?

BURKE

Yes.

As Harry Wildair, wearing a boy's dress
With youthful swagger! Lovely! Debonair!
The darling of the wits!

WOFFINGTON

(dryly: with malice).

Then I dare swear
You've never seen her in her right clothes?

BURKE

No.

Not yet.

WOFFINGTON

But, sir——

BURKE

The times are hard, and so——
*(He looks down regretfully at his shabby clothes, and
      makes a rueful gesture.)*
When I've more silver I shall go each night.

WOFFINGTON

(with deep conviction).

You'd spend your good coin on a worthless sight.
She's just an actress. *(She manages to keep her hands
      in the shadow.)*

BURKE
(quietly).
Tell me what you mean.

WOFFINGTON
(with the proper amount of hesitation).
Well, on the stage, sir, she may be a queen,
But off the stage——! A zany, underbred,
Without a scrap of learning in her head.

BURKE
(indignantly).
And I suppose her beauty's false as well?

WOFFINGTON
Sure, they do say (though you can never tell!)
That underneath the powder and the paint
You'll find a—*something that is not a saint*.

BURKE
(furious).
Be silent!

[*He rises, pale with anger.*

WOFFINGTON
Oh, is Woffington your friend?
Sure, sir, I had no meaning to offend.

BURKE

(more quietly).

Peg Woffington is not a friend of mine.
I saw her once upon the stage. So fine,
So true an artist that the gossips slur
Her name through arrant jealousy of her

(With growing power.)

Who is as far above them as the light
Of the first stars. Her genius burns as bright
As does Orion. Can you look at her——

WOFFINGTON

(to herself).

(I often do!)

BURKE

(sweeping on, unheeding).

——without a great heart-stir
Of Irish pride, to think what high renown
Is worn by lovely Peg of Dublin town?

*(All the fire that will one day be his flames through
his words.)*

From Ireland, land of all that's brave and sweet. . . .

WOFFINGTON

(provocatively).

Famed for its lawyers, actresses, and—peat!

(He turns from her indignantly.)

Sure, don't be angry. I am Irish, too.

BURKE

(turning on her).

Take shame, then, to yourself, to think that you
Speak lightly of Peg Woffington——

WOFFINGTON

*(suddenly standing up, returning to her natural voice
and manner, and tossing off his cloak so that the
black and silver and scarlet of her costume shows
up wondrously in the candlelight).*

Nay, hold!
I think I know all that I need be told!
I'll choose the one who can defend me best!

BURKE

(with icy pride).

Madam, I'm glad that we have proved a jest
To pass your time, my poverty and I.

WOFFINGTON

(with a cry).

How can you think that!

BURKE

(bowing sardonically).

And the moments fly
When one is well amused. I trust that you
Have spent your evening profitably. Do
Remember me at court. *(He bows again.)*

WOFFINGTON

I shall, sir!

[*They have been too engrossed with their own
emotions to notice Greville, who has opened
the window and stepped in.*

GREVILLE

Peg,

I've brought your chair.

BURKE

(*suddenly looking at her indignantly*).

You said your name was Meg.

WOFFINGTON

(*with a return of her gamin accent*).

Well, Meg or Peg, 'tis very much the same:
And even Shakespeare says: " What's in a name? "

(*Again the fine lady.*)

Mr. Burke, Mr. Greville.

(*Stiff bows. Woffington indicates Burke.*)

He's the one

Who's to be lawyer for Peg Woffington. (*Indicates
herself.*)

BURKE

(*staring at her, fascinated*).

Peg Woffington—you don't mean——

WOFFINGTON
(laughing).

Man, you're blind!
I'm Peg!

(She sweeps him a curtsey.)

BURKE

And I, who said you were unkind
To mock me——

WOFFINGTON

Find a client here instead!
The suit's against Miss Spleen. Say what you said
To Meg, the crossing sweeper, and all will be well.
Good night.

[*Greville pauses, waiting for her at the window.*

BURKE

(gazing at her).

Good night. Your beauty's like a spell
That holds thanks tongue-tied.

WOFFINGTON

(drolly).

Wouldn't you have known
We both kissed Ireland's gem—the Blarney Stone.

(Curtseys.)

Good night, then.

[*The men bow to each other, and Woffington
starts to join Greville. Then turns impetu-
ously, runs back to the table, tears the crim-
son rose from her dress, kisses it lightly and
tosses it to the table with a charming gesture.*

Here's success! And great renown!

[*She runs back, and exits hastily by way of the
window, Greville following. Burke stands
for an instant looking after her. Then he
lifts the rose to his lips.*

BURKE

Peg Woffington! The rose of Dublin Town.

[*He stands, smiling dreamily at the rose as the
curtain falls.*

THE PRINCE OF COURT PAINTERS

George Romney

From the portrait by himself

THE PRINCE OF COURT PAINTERS

CHARACTERS

GEORGE ROMNEY (the Prince of Court Painters)
MARY ROMNEY, his wife
LUCY ELRIDGE, a neighbor's child.
>PLACE: *A village in the north of England.*
>TIME: *1799.*
>SCENE: *Mary Romney's home.*

The living-room of a peasant-like cottage which, with its dark floor and walls of time-stained wood, and its great rafters, suggests the seventeenth rather than the eighteenth century.

In center background a dark oak door opens on a wild bit of moorland stretching towards the western skyline. On each side of this door long narrow latticed windows swinging inward, and curtained with faintly flowered muslin.

At left a wide-mouthed hearth built of cobblestones. Iron andirons and an iron kettle on a hob. On the hearthshelf candles in pewter candlesticks, and a plate or two. Everywhere simplicity and frugality is manifest. A dark wooden settle by fire, facing audience.

A dark-stained table in the center of the room. It

is round, and made of plain wood.   There are also in other parts of the room some quaint sturdy chairs of dark wood set against the wall.

Against the right wall a dark oak cupboard, containing earthenware dishes, and a little food—such as a loaf of wheaten bread, butter, cheese, and honey.   Beyond this a churn, and a spinning wheel for Mary Romney's use.

At the rise of the curtain a low fire is burning on the hearth, and through the open door and western windows the light of late afternoon shines on Mary Romney as she sits at her spinning wheel, right.   She is not a young woman, but age has touched her lightly. Her figure is still straight and supple.   Her snow-white hair only adds to the charming effect of the ivory pallor of her face.   Her eyes have retained their look of youth, of a spirit that is never done hoping.   There is about her an air of gentle strength.   She wears a dress of dove-gray homespun, with a white linen kerchief crossed on her breast.   She has no trinkets or adornments of any kind, and needs none.   As the curtain rises she is singing, her voice blending pleasantly with the hum of the wheel:

MARY ROMNEY

Rest!   Rest!   Twilight is best.   The day's storms die. Sleep.   Sleep.   White stars will keep their watch on high.

> [*While Mary Romney sings, Lucy Elridge appears on the threshold.   She is a small child*

of seven or eight years. She wears a high-
waisted frock of white muslin, plainly made,
and white stockings with low black slippers
laced with black ribbon above her ankles.
On her head a mob cap of white swiss. She
carries a little wicker basket with flowers
in it.

MARY ROMNEY
(rising).

Come in.

LUCY
(entering).

What do you sing?

MARY ROMNEY
A lullaby
That sends tired children off to sleep.

LUCY
(presenting flowers).
You've none,
You live alone—away from everyone.
But I love you.   And that is why I came.

MARY ROMNEY
Thank you, dear Lucy.

LUCY

                    And I love your name.
Just "Mary Romney."   *(Dwells on it musically.)*
        I've heard people say
That someone married you, and went away.
His name was Romney, too.   And then you left
The place where you were living.

MARY ROMNEY

                              What a weft
Do gossips weave!   With what threads is it strung!

LUCY

(innocently sage).

It happened long ago, when you were young.
I heard it all.   Something to you was sent.
And since that time both food and warmth you've spent
On the world's poor.   Who are the world's poor?

MARY ROMNEY

(quietly).

                                    Those
To whom life gives the thorn, but not the rose.

LUCY

I do not understand.

MARY ROMNEY

            How should you, dear.

LUCY

(coaxingly, leaning against Mary Romney's knee).

Tell me about " When you were young."

MARY ROMNEY

I fear

I cannot.   *(Staring before her.)*   Why, to think of
    such a thing
Is like a dream.   Black as the raven's wing
My hair was then.

LUCY

And were your cheeks as pink

As Mother's are?

MARY ROMNEY

Yes.   Is it strange to think

That I was young once?   Ah, time's wind can blow
The reddest roses into flowers of snow.

LUCY

(puzzled).

Like Winter?

MARY ROMNEY

Aye.

LUCY

(innocently).

Was he—was Romney old

And cross like Gaffer Matthew?   Did he scold?

MARY ROMNEY
(deeply).

No.

(She forgets Lucy. Her face is lit by an inner flame.)

He was young—young as the morning star,
And blithe as Spring.   *(With sudden quiet.)*   But,
    child, those days are far.
Too far to talk about.

(Lucy turns reluctantly and takes her basket.)
Dear, must you go?

LUCY

My Mother says my feet are always slow
Upon the homeward way.

[*Mary Romney crosses to cupboard, takes out
    a pat of butter and a little tart.*

MARY ROMNEY
(indicating Lucy's basket).
Child, will this hold
A little pat of butter, bright as gold,
And a small tart?

LUCY
I thank you.

MARY ROMNEY
Now run home.
I would not have you linger through the gloam.

[*She kisses Lucy, who exits sedately, carrying
    her basket.   For a moment Mary Romney*

leans by the door watching her, then she re-
turns to her wheel. The light of afternoon
has faded into the glow of sunset. As Mary
Romney sits at her wheel a shadow falls
across the doorway. She looks up and sees
a slim dark man, worn, but not bent with
age. His hair is grizzled, and hangs loosely
about his pale passionate face. He wears a
weatherworn black cloak and black suit. A
broad felt hat, with dilapidated brim, a very
scarecrow of a hat. From under its brim
the haunted eyes of the man look out like
the eyes of a lost soul. Fatigue, hunger, de-
spair have set their thumb-mark on him. He
belongs to the Lost Legion of the world.
Under his arm he carries a battered port-
folio of black leather worn gray with time
and exposure. No one would ever guess this
apparition to be Romney. Least of all does
Romney's wife guess it. Too many years
have come and gone since their last meeting.

ROMNEY

Could you give shelter to a traveler
So worn and weary that he scarce can stir
Another foot along the road?
　　　(Mary rises and looks at him pityingly.)
　　　　　　　　　　　　　　I fear
That I have startled you. And yet—look clear
And see what begs a refuge! Bone and shred
Can scarce work harm to any. *(He coughs.)*

MARY ROMNEY
(with swift compassion).

Warmed and fed
You shall be.

ROMNEY

Thank you—greatly.

[*He crosses weakly to the fire. Mary crosses to the cupboard and brings him a plate of bread and a cup of cordial.*

MARY ROMNEY

Sit you down.
Often do folk pass by here from the town,
Early and late, and though I live alone
I never have had cause to fear.

ROMNEY
(sits, leaning back, spent).

A stone
Is what the world gives when you ask for bread;
Yet you give this——

MARY ROMNEY

Eat, and be comforted.
(Cheerily.)
"Darkest before the dawn" the old wives say.

ROMNEY

I am a traveler who has lost his way,
And followed ignus fatuus till the night
Closed in on me, and left me without light.

MARY ROMNEY
(to herself).

He wanders.

ROMNEY
(half-hearing her).

Aye. Oh, I have wandered far,
And though the dancing wisp-light was a star,
The light called *" Art."*

MARY ROMNEY

You are an artist? *(He bows.)* Then
You must have heard of him! *(Her voice thrills with
pride.)*

ROMNEY
Him?

MARY ROMNEY

Whom all men
Praise. The great Romney. *(The name transfigures
her.)*

ROMNEY

He is great no more.
Why, I have heard he goes from door to door
Glad of a little charity.

MARY ROMNEY
(proudly).

You err.
He is the prince of all court painters, sir.
His friends are lords and duchesses.

ROMNEY

They slip
From him as rats desert a rotting ship
That's settling down and down.

MARY ROMNEY
(torn).

Is this thing true?

ROMNEY
(his haunted eyes on her).

Should I give falsehood as a coin to you
Who are so kind?

MARY ROMNEY
(passionately).

Where is he?

ROMNEY

Who can say.

MARY ROMNEY

Had he no wife?

ROMNEY

In some far yesterday
I think he had. But when Sir Joshua said:
" Forget your country marriage, and instead
Take Art to wife," he left her. Well, his art
Brought fame and money; but his secret heart
Like a closed house, was haunted by a ghost. . . .

MARY ROMNEY
(quietly).
Yet there were other women.

ROMNEY
(wearily).
Oh, a host
Of frilled and furbelowed great ladies. . . .

MARY ROMNEY
One
Of these was called the Lady Hamilton,
Was she not? *(She lights a candle on the mantle-shelf.)*

ROMNEY
Yes.

MARY ROMNEY
And he loved her?

ROMNEY
Her face
Bewitched the artist in him, and her grace
Filled many a canvas.

MARY ROMNEY
And he loved her.

ROMNEY

(rousing himself).

No.

He loved her beauty.   (With renewed quiet.)   That
    was long ago,
And all of it is like a tale that's told.

(Bitterly.)

Only one love did Romney's bleak heart hold
And her he wronged.

MARY ROMNEY

And will he not return?

ROMNEY

(wryly).

And say, " My wife, whose love I seemed to spurn,
You did not share in my celebrity;
But now I'm old and poor.   Pray comfort me."

(For an instant his face lights sardonically.)

I think that Romney would not fall so low
For all his faults.

MARY ROMNEY

Does he—does Romney know
Where his wife lives?

ROMNEY

Nay.   Somewhere in the North.
He's lost all trace. *(Rises.)* 'Tis time that I set forth
Ere night falls utterly.
(He opens his portfolio, fumbles in it, takes out a
sketch.)

I pray you take
A little sketch, such as I used to make.
'Tis all the coin I have. *(He coughs.)*

MARY ROMNEY
(amazed).

'Tis finely done.
Aye, wondrous fine!

[*Before he has grasped what she is doing she*
takes another picture from the portfolio, the
rosy portrait of a young and beautiful coun-
try girl.

Oh, let me see this one!

ROMNEY

A sketch of Romney's wife, made by himself
From memory.   Life-sized.

MARY ROMNEY
(stooping at hearth and taking money from under loose
stone).

Beneath this shelf
I have ten pounds and more.   Sell this to me.
(As if in explanation of her strange conduct.)
It is so young!   So fair!

ROMNEY

(looking at it with the enthrallment of the artist).

It cannot be.
I cannot sell it. It is Romney's wife.
Painted from memory. And true to life
Each contour that I loved.

MARY ROMNEY

You loved!

ROMNEY

Yes, I

Am Romney.

[*He looks at the picture as if held by a spell.
For all that he sees or hears he is alone in
the room.*

MARY ROMNEY

Romney!

ROMNEY

Why, with what a cry

You speak my name.

[*They gaze at each other in the dim light.*

MARY ROMNEY

Mine also.

[*She faces him steadily. Romney snatches up
the candle, looks at her. Puts it down.*

ROMNEY

God is just.
He leads me, old and humble, in the dust
Before your door——

> [*His head is bowed for an instant. He cannot
> look at her. Slowly, and with dread, he
> raises his eyes, and meets her answering look,
> her gesture towards him. Speaks brokenly,
> uncertainly.*

I, who should be reviled. . . .
You can forgive me. . . .

MARY ROMNEY

(with beautiful maternal tenderness).

Why, you are my child.
My genius child, who all day long must roam,
And then at twilight sees the lights of home.

ROMNEY

Mary!

MARY ROMNEY

I ask no question of the past.
What was mine at the first is now mine last.

ROMNEY

(still brokenly: to himself).

" And ministering angels came to bless——"
Ah, but I have no right—— *(Yet his eyes implore
her.)*

MARY ROMNEY

After day's stress

Comes peace and twilight. Look, where the last bar
Of sunset fades, the steadfast evening star!

> [*Through the last rose of sunset and the gathering violet of dusk the white glimmer of the evening star is seen through the open doorway. Mary Romney, her hand on Romney's shoulder, watches it, and with a half breath sings very low and soothingly, her voice a crooning murmur:*

Rest! Rest! Twilight is best. The day's storms die.

ROMNEY

What do you sing?

MARY ROMNEY

(with ineffable tenderness).

A tired child's lullaby.

> [*The music of the song is faintly continued by the orchestra as the curtain falls.*

CLARK'S CONTINENTAL DRAMA OF TO-DAY—Outlines for Its Study

By BARRETT H. CLARK, Editor of and Translator of two of the plays in "Three Modern French Plays." 12mo. $1.35 net.

Suggestions, questions, biographies, and bibliographies for use in connection with the study of some of the more important plays of IBSEN, BJÖRNSEN, STRINDBERG, TOLSTOY, GORKY, TCHEKOFF, ANDREYEFF, HAUPTMANN, SUDERMANN, WEDEKIND, SCHNITZLER, VON HOFFMANSTHAL, BECQUE, LE MAÎTRE, LAVEDAN, DONNAY, MAETERLINCK, ROSTAND, BRIEUX, HERVIEU, GIACOSA, D'ANNUNZIO, ECHEGARAY, and GALDOS.

In half a dozen or less pages for each play, Mr. Clark tries to indicate, in a way suggestive to playwriters and students, how the skilled dramatists write their plays. It is intended that the volume shall be used in connection with the reading of the plays themselves, but it also has an independent interest in itself.

Prof. William Lyon Phelps of Yale: ". . . One of the most useful works on the contemporary drama. . . . Extremely practical, full of valuable hints and suggestions. . . ."

Providence Journal: "Of undoubted value. . . . At the completion of a study of the plays in connection with the 'Outline' one should have a definite knowledge of the essentials of dramatic technique in general, and of the modern movement in particular."

Sixth Edition, Enlarged and with Portraits

HALE'S DRAMATIST'S OF TO-DAY

By PROF. EDWARD EVERETT HALE, JR., of Union College.

ROSTAND, HAUPTMANN, SUDERMANN,
PINERO, SHAW, PHILLIPS, MAETERLINCK

"A Note on Standards of Criticism," "Our Idea of Tragedy," and an appendix of all the plays of each author, with dates of their first performance or publication, complete the volume. $1.50 net.

New York Evening Post: "It is not often nowadays that a theatrical book can be met with so free from gush and mere eulogy, or so weighted by common sense . . . an excellent chronological appendix and full index . . . uncommonly useful for reference."

Brooklyn Eagle: "A dramatic critic who is not just 'busting' himself with Titanic intellectualities, but who is a readable dramatic critic. . . . Mr. Hale is a modest and sensible, as well as an acute and sound critic. . . . Most people will be surprised and delighted with Mr. Hale's simplicity, perspicuity and ingenuousness."

HENRY HOLT AND COMPANY

PUBLISHERS   NEW YORK